D1081420

Written by Neil Morris

Cartoons by Mark Davis

Projects created by
Ting Morris

Art direction
Clare Sleven

Design
Mackerel Design

Project management
Mark Darling

Artwork commissioned by
Lynne French, Susanne Grant, Natasha Smith

Art reference
Lesley Cartlidge, Liberty Mella

Editorial director
Paula Borton

First published in 2000 by
Miles Kelly Publishing Ltd
Bardfield Centre, Great Bardfield, Essex CM7 4SL
Reprinted 2001

2468109753

Copyright © Miles Kelly Publishing Ltd 2000

All rights reserved. No part of this publication may be reproduced, stored in a retrieval system, or transmitted by any means, electronic, mechanical, photocopying, recording or otherwise, without the prior permission of the copyright holder.

British Library Cataloguing-in-Publication Data
A catalogue record for this book is available from the British Library

ISBN 1-90294-736-3

Printed in Hong Kong

Acknowledgements

The publishers wish to thank the following artists who have contributed to this book:
Mark Davis (Mackerel Design), Terry Gabbey (AFA),
Richard Hook (Linden Artists), John James (Temple Rogers),
Janos Marffy, Guy Smith (Mainline Design),
Mike White (Temple Rogers), John Woodcock.

The publishers wish to thank the following sources for the photographs used in this book:
Stock Market: Page 16 (L), 17 (TR)
Corbis: Page 21(M), 45 (TL), 46 (M), 47 (BL)
All other photographs from Miles Kelly Archives.

e-mail: info@mileskelly.net
www.mileskelly.net

CONTENTS

THE WORLD'S ENVIRONMENTS

Where people live and the way in which they live depend on the different environments that make up our world. These environments, or surroundings, include evergreen forests (where the trees keep their leaves all year round), deciduous forests (where the trees drop their leaves in the autumn), rainforests, grasslands, mountains and deserts. It is cold and icy in the regions near the North and South Poles.

Evergreen forests of Northern Europe

Mountains in Peru

Rainforest in Brazil

Quiz

1 Which is the largest continent?

2 Which type of forest do pine trees grow in?

3 Which continent has no people living on it permanently?

4 Is an apple tree deciduous or evergreen?

5 Which river runs through the world's biggest rainforest?

6 Which is the smallest continent?

Answers
1 Asia. 2 Evergreen. 3 Antarctica.
4 Deciduous. 5 Amazon. 6 Australasia.

Deserts of North Africa

Find their way home

Can you match the people to their homes? One comes from a very cold environment, another from the plains, and the third lives in a big city. Which home is left as the odd one out?

A.

B.   C.   D.

Answers
1.C 2.D 3.A
B is the odd one out!

1.   2.   3.

Grasslands of central Africa

Polar region of Antarctica

PEOPLE TRADITIONALLY BUILD HOMES OF LOCAL MATERIALS.

Factfile

- The world's land is divided into seven continents: Africa, Antarctica, Asia, Australasia, Europe, North America and South America.

- The area around the North Pole is called the Arctic; it is covered by the Arctic Ocean, which is frozen at the surface.

- The area around the South Pole is the continent of Antarctica, where the land is permanently covered by ice and snow.

- Deserts cover about one seventh of the Earth's surface.

NORTH AMERICA

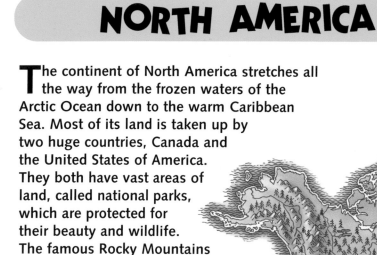

The continent of North America stretches all the way from the frozen waters of the Arctic Ocean down to the warm Caribbean Sea. Most of its land is taken up by two huge countries, Canada and the United States of America. They both have vast areas of land, called national parks, which are protected for their beauty and wildlife. The famous Rocky Mountains run almost all the way down the western side of the continent.

Factfile

- The Trans-Canada Highway stretches right across Canada for about 8,000 km.

- Lake Superior is the largest freshwater lake in the world.

- The famous Niagara Falls have two main waterfalls: the 49 m high Horseshoe Falls are in Canada; and the 51 m high American Falls are in the USA.

- The city of Chicago got its name from a Native American word for "place where wild onions grow".

The Grand Canyon is 350 km long and up to 2 km deep – the largest gorge in the world.

Prairies are large areas of flat grassland in Canada and the USA.

Quiz

1 In which American state is the Grand Canyon – Arizona, Florida or Wisconsin?

2 Which is the biggest of the Great Lakes?

3 What is the capital of the USA?

4 Which river flows over the Niagara Falls?

5 What is the name of the canal that joins the Pacific and Atlantic Oceans?

6 Canada is bigger than the USA – true or false?

Answers
1 Arizona. 2 Lake Superior 3 Washington D.C.
4 Niagara River. 5 Panama Canal.
6 True.

THE ELEVATOR'S BROKEN DOWN!

Make a teepee

LARGE STRAWS

1. You'll need four cut-off garden sticks or large straws for the poles (about 20 cm long). Tie each set of two sticks in the form of an X, but with the cross-over point close to the top. Place one X over the other so that the cross-over points rest on each other. Bind the two together.

2. For the teepee shape draw a circle around a 20 cm wide plate on card, cut it out and then cut it in half. Paint your own pattern and cut out two door-holes.

3. Put the painted teepee shape round the sticks and close it with sticky tape or a card tab. Trim the sticks level with the bottom of the teepee.

7

ORTH AMERICA PEOPLE

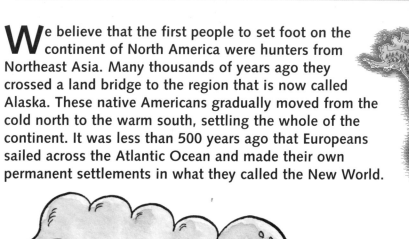

We believe that the first people to set foot on the continent of North America were hunters from Northeast Asia. Many thousands of years ago they crossed a land bridge to the region that is now called Alaska. These native Americans gradually moved from the cold north to the warm south, settling the whole of the continent. It was less than 500 years ago that Europeans sailed across the Atlantic Ocean and made their own permanent settlements in what they called the New World.

Factfile

• The Inuit live in northern Canada and Greenland; they have their own homeland in Canada, called Nunavut (meaning "Our Land").

• The CN Tower in Toronto, Canada, is the world's tallest free-standing structure; it is 553 m high.

• The largest cities on the continent are New York, Mexico City and Los Angeles.

• The Aztecs of Mexico had their capital at Tenochtitlan; it was destroyed by Spanish conquerors in 1521 and Mexico City was built on top of the ruins.

This stepped pyramid temple was found at the Mayan city of Chichen Itza, in Mexico. The Mayan civilization flourished in Mexico, Guatemala and Belize from about AD300 to 900.

Cowboys ride bucking broncos at festivals of horsemanship called rodeos. The cowboy tries to stay on for as long as he can.

Quiz

1 The USA has about five times as many people as Canada – true or false?

2 In which month do Americans celebrate Thanksgiving?

3 What is the capital of Canada?

4 What is the top American football match called?

5 Which American state has most people?

6 Is New England in Canada, the UK or the USA?

Answers
1 False (it has about nine times as many). 2 November 3 Ottawa. 4 Super Bowl. 5 California. 6 USA.

HUT, HUT!

Feather head-dress

FEATHER

CARD

1. Cut a strip of corrugated paper (55 cm x 6 cm) and fit the strip around your head. Glue on crunched-up tissue-paper decorations, painted pasta shapes and leaves. Stick the ends together with parcel tape.

2. Collect real feathers. You can make your own by cutting out pieces of coloured tissue paper about 18 cm long. Glue the feathers onto thin plastic straws, leaving space at the bottom of each straw. Snip fringes into the feathers as shown and push them into the holes of the corrugated paper strip.

3. Now your head-dress is ready to wear.

SOUTH AMERICA

Brazil is by far the largest of the 13 countries that make up South America. It covers nearly half the continent's area. The world's longest range of mountains, the Andes, stretch down the western side of the continent. The River Amazon rises high up in the Andes of Peru. It flows for about 6,500 km through the world's largest rainforest, on its way to the Atlantic Ocean.

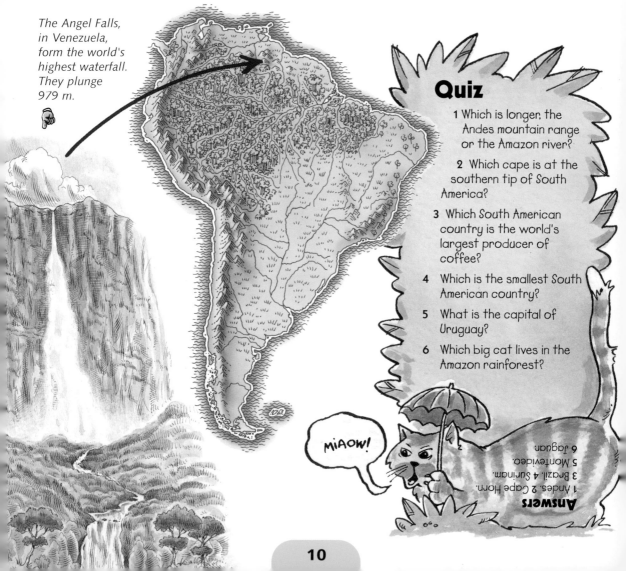

The Angel Falls, in Venezuela, form the world's highest waterfall. They plunge 979 m.

Quiz

1 Which is longer, the Andes mountain range or the Amazon river?

2 Which cape is at the southern tip of South America?

3 Which South American country is the world's largest producer of coffee?

4 Which is the smallest South American country?

5 What is the capital of Uruguay?

6 Which big cat lives in the Amazon rainforest?

MiAOW!

Answers
1 Andes. 2 Cape Horn.
3 Brazil. 4 Surinam.
5 Montevideo. 6 Jaguar.

Factfile

- There are more than 2,000 kinds of fish in the Amazon, including the deadly piranha.

- The Atacama Desert stretches for almost 1,000 km along the Pacific coast of Chile; the desert is very rich in minerals.

- The Amazon rainforest covers about six million sq. km across parts of nine countries.

- The name Brazil comes from the Portuguese for "red wood dye".

- The world's largest open-cast copper mine is in Chile; the giant hole in the ground measures 4.8 km by 2.5 km.

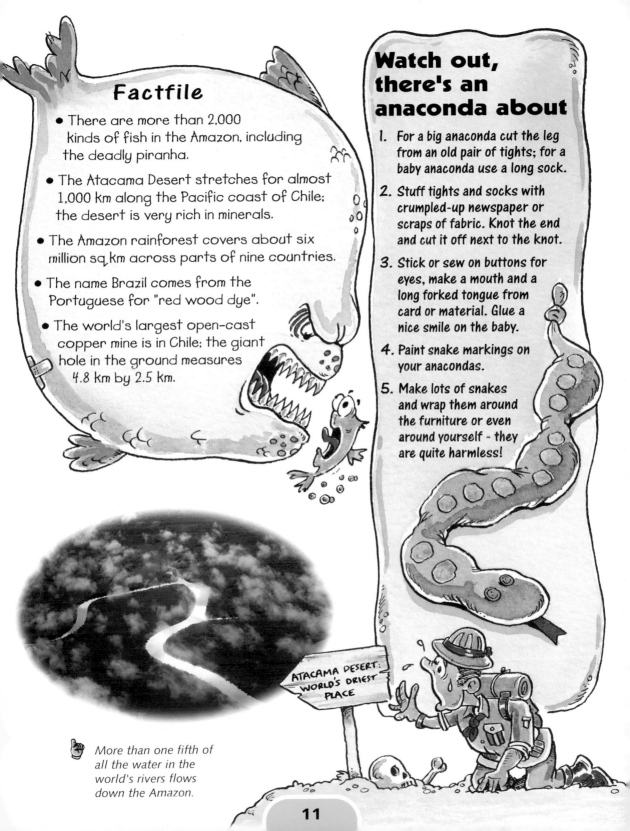

ATACAMA DESERT: WORLD'S DRIEST PLACE

More than one fifth of all the water in the world's rivers flows down the Amazon.

Watch out, there's an anaconda about

1. For a big anaconda cut the leg from an old pair of tights; for a baby anaconda use a long sock.

2. Stuff tights and socks with crumpled-up newspaper or scraps of fabric. Knot the end and cut it off next to the knot.

3. Stick or sew on buttons for eyes, make a mouth and a long forked tongue from card or material. Glue a nice smile on the baby.

4. Paint snake markings on your anacondas.

5. Make lots of snakes and wrap them around the furniture or even around yourself - they are quite harmless!

SOUTH AMERICAN PEOPLE

Native American cultures had flourished for thousands of years when the first Europeans arrived in South America in the 1500s. Most of today's South Americans are descended from native Americans and Europeans, and many are a mixture of the two. Spanish is the continent's main language, except in Brazil, where people speak Portuguese. Native Americans still speak hundreds of Indian languages.

Gauchos herd cattle, making Argentina one of the world's biggest beef producers.

Factfile

- Lake Titicaca is the highest navigable lake in the world, at 3,811 m above sea level.

- Soccer is the most popular sport in South America; Brazil has won the World Cup four times.

- The mighty Inca empire once ruled over the Andes region from their capital city of Cuzco, in Peru.

- The Yanomami are the largest Amazonian forest tribe, but there are only about 19,000 of them left.

THIS IS EASY WITHOUT A GOALKEEPER!

Aymara people build reed boats to sail on Lake Titicaca, between Peru and Bolivia.

Quiz

1 What is the capital of Brazil?

2 In which century did European explorers first reach South America?

3 Which country staged the first ever soccer World Cup?

4 Potatoes come originally from the Andes region– true or false?

5 The highest mountain in the Andes is Aconcagua – which country is it in?

6 Where is La Paz, the world's highest capital city?

Answers
1 Brasilia. 2 The 15th century. 3 Uruguay 4 True. 5 Argentina. 6 Bolivia.

Rio carnival shakers

1. All you need is four yoghurt pots, dried peas and beans, some masking tape, sweet wrappers and coloured foil or paper for decoration.

2. Put the beans into one pot, then join it together with another pot using masking tape.

3. Glue on the sweet wrappers or cut-up pieces of coloured paper and foil.

4. Make another shaker in the same way and fill it with the peas to vary the sound.

5. Hold one in each hand and shake away!

EUROPE

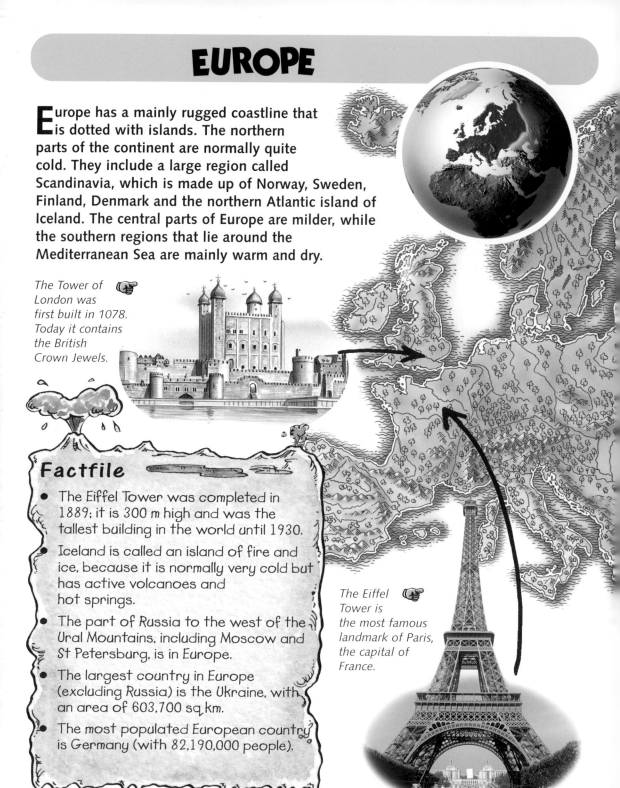

Europe has a mainly rugged coastline that is dotted with islands. The northern parts of the continent are normally quite cold. They include a large region called Scandinavia, which is made up of Norway, Sweden, Finland, Denmark and the northern Atlantic island of Iceland. The central parts of Europe are milder, while the southern regions that lie around the Mediterranean Sea are mainly warm and dry.

The Tower of London was first built in 1078. Today it contains the British Crown Jewels.

Factfile

- The Eiffel Tower was completed in 1889; it is 300 m high and was the tallest building in the world until 1930.

- Iceland is called an island of fire and ice, because it is normally very cold but has active volcanoes and hot springs.

- The part of Russia to the west of the Ural Mountains, including Moscow and St Petersburg, is in Europe.

- The largest country in Europe (excluding Russia) is the Ukraine, with an area of 603,700 sq km.

- The most populated European country is Germany (with 82,190,000 people).

The Eiffel Tower is the most famous landmark of Paris, the capital of France.

Build a junk town

1. Collect together lots of small cardboard boxes for your houses. Cereal packets make good skyscrapers. Use a large cardboard lid or piece of card for the base.

2. Mark out roads, a park and spaces for your houses with a pencil. Paint the roads grey and the park and gardens green. Paint the boxes to look like houses with doors and windows. Cut some card to make the roofs. Stick together a number of small boxes to make blocks of flats, a supermarket, a school and a church. Arrange all the houses on the base. Make some trees from twigs stuck in plasticine.

Quiz

1. Which continent is the non-European part of Russia in?

2. The Black Sea's water is black – true or false?

3. Which is larger, Norway or Sweden?

4. In which city are the ancient Forum and Colosseum?

5. Which sea's name means "in the middle of the earth"?

6. Which three countries make up Benelux?

OH, NO!!

Answers

1 Asia. 2 False (it's greeny blue). 3 Sweden. 4 Rome. 5 Mediterranean. 6 Belgium, the Netherlands and Luxembourg.

EUROPEAN PEOPLE

Europe is full of many small countries and different peoples. Most have different cultures and customs, but they also have a lot in common. The northern Scandinavians are descendants of the Vikings. Further south, the French, Spanish and Italian languages all came from Latin, the language of the ancient Romans. Ancient Greek and Roman civilizations influenced European ideas of art, philosophy and law.

Flamenco is a traditional way of dancing and singing to guitar music that is very popular in Spain.

Make a Spanish fan

1. Take a long sheet of paper and paint a bright pattern on it. Then decorate it with glitter glue.

2. When it's dry, fold the sheet into a concertina, keeping the folds all the same size. Staple the folds together at one end and attach this to a lolly stick for a handle.

3. Now you can keep cool with your fancy Spanish fan.

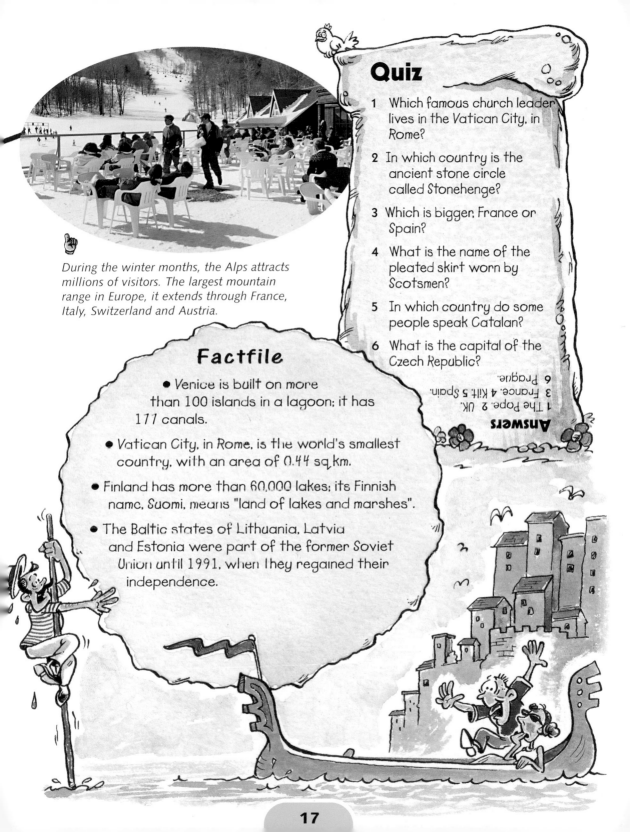

During the winter months, the Alps attracts millions of visitors. The largest mountain range in Europe, it extends through France, Italy, Switzerland and Austria.

Quiz

1. Which famous church leader lives in the Vatican City, in Rome?

2. In which country is the ancient stone circle called Stonehenge?

3. Which is bigger, France or Spain?

4. What is the name of the pleated skirt worn by Scotsmen?

5. In which country do some people speak Catalan?

6. What is the capital of the Czech Republic?

Answers
1 The Pope. 2 UK.
3 France. 4 Kilt 5 Spain.
6 Prague.

Factfile

- Venice is built on more than 100 islands in a lagoon; it has 177 canals.

- Vatican City, in Rome, is the world's smallest country, with an area of 0.44 sq km.

- Finland has more than 60,000 lakes; its Finnish name, Suomi, means "land of lakes and marshes".

- The Baltic states of Lithuania, Latvia and Estonia were part of the former Soviet Union until 1991, when they regained their independence.

ASIA

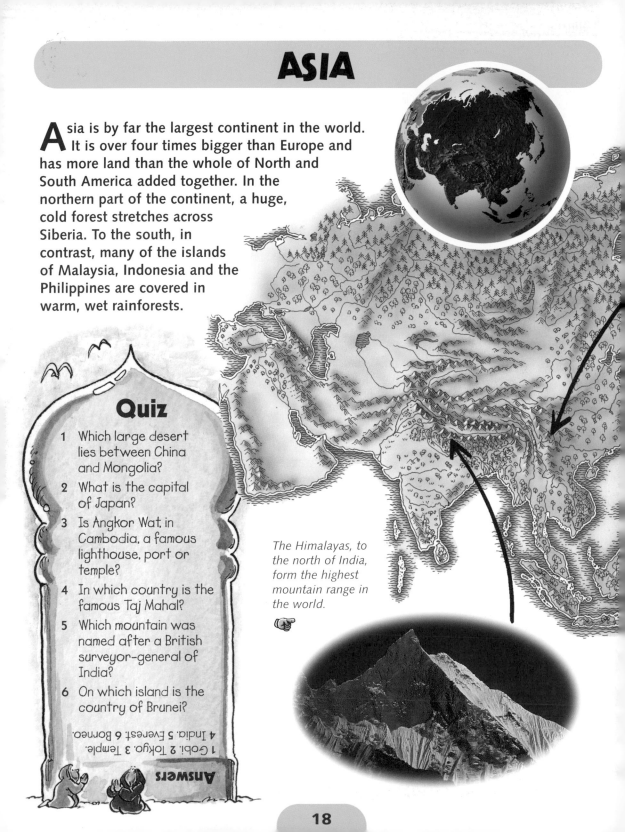

Asia is by far the largest continent in the world. It is over four times bigger than Europe and has more land than the whole of North and South America added together. In the northern part of the continent, a huge, cold forest stretches across Siberia. To the south, in contrast, many of the islands of Malaysia, Indonesia and the Philippines are covered in warm, wet rainforests.

Quiz

1 Which large desert lies between China and Mongolia?

2 What is the capital of Japan?

3 Is Angkor Wat, in Cambodia, a famous lighthouse, port or temple?

4 In which country is the famous Taj Mahal?

5 Which mountain was named after a British surveyor-general of India?

6 On which island is the country of Brunei?

4 India 5 Everest 6 Borneo.
1 Gobi 2 Tokyo 3 Temple.
Answers

The Himalayas, to the north of India, form the highest mountain range in the world.

18

- The Japanese tea ceremony has been handed down from ancient times, and is still used to show grace and good manners.

- Mount Everest, in the Himalayas, is the world's highest mountain, at 8,848 m.

- Altogether, the Great Wall of China is about 6,400 km long; it used to be said that it could be seen from the Moon but lunar astronauts disagree.

- Japan's most famous mountain, Fuji, is a sacred volcano that last erupted in 1707.

The Great Wall of China was first built over 2,000 years ago, to keep out invaders from the north.

JUST TRY TO CLEAN IT UP GRACEFULLY!

Japanese flower arrangement

1. It's easy to make a simple arrangement in a see-through bowl.

2. Put soil at the bottom of the bowl, and add gravel, shells and pebbles. Now push a small twig through the gravel into the soil.

3. Half-fill the bowl with water and decorate the surface with pretty leaves and flowers (real or paper).

This is simple Asian beauty.

ASIAN PEOPLE

The world's first civilizations grew up in Southwest Asia. Early wandering people first settled in the fertile region between two great rivers, the Euphrates and the Tigris. They started to grow crops and eventually built cities. Today, more than half the world's people live in Asia. This continent also includes the country with more people than any other, China. This was an important and powerful empire in ancient times.

Factfile

- The first people to climb Mount Everest were a Nepalese Sherpa called Tenzing Norgay and a New Zealander named Edmund Hillary, in 1953.

- Sherpa people live in some of the highest villages in the world, in the Himalayas. They are farmers and herders, as well as skilled mountaineers.

- The Sultan of Brunei, one of the world's richest men, has a palace with 1,788 rooms.

- The Petronas Towers in Kuala Lumpur, the capital of Malaysia, form the world's tallest building; the twin towers are 452 m high.

Floating markets in Thailand make it easy to transport produce.

Weave a Persian rug

Ancient Persians made the most beautiful rugs, now you can too!

1. Fold 12 double-pages of newspaper into strips. Fold each sheet in half lengthways, then fold it in half twice more and press each strip to flatten it out.

2. Place six strips side by side to form an even edge, and tape them down so they stay in position. Weave the other six strips over and under the strips you taped down, as shown. The first, third and fifth strips go over and under.

The second, fourth and sixth strips go under and over.

3. Untape the strips and push the rows together, moving the strips until the ends are even all around the rug. Fold the loose ends of the strips over and tuck them in.

PAPER STRIPS

Japanese sumo wrestlers are big and very strong. They try to throw their opponent down or force him out of the ring.

I THINK I'M GOING TO NEED A LONGER LADDER!

Petronas Towers

Quiz

1 How many islands make up the Philippines, 7, 70, 700 or 7,000?

2 What is the capital of Thailand?

3 Chinese New Year is on 1 January – true or false?

4 Which country does the island of Honshu belong to?

5 Which country was named after King Philip II of Spain?

6 Which country does Hong Kong belong to?

Answers

1 7000. 2 Bangkok.
3 False (it's between 21 January and 20 February). 4 Japan.
5 Philippines. 6 China.

AFRICA

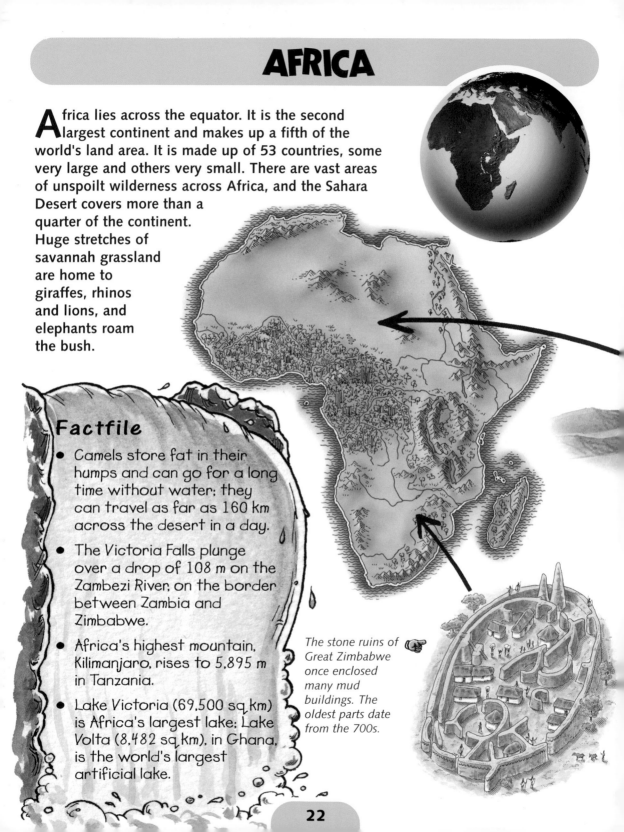

Africa lies across the equator. It is the second largest continent and makes up a fifth of the world's land area. It is made up of 53 countries, some very large and others very small. There are vast areas of unspoilt wilderness across Africa, and the Sahara Desert covers more than a quarter of the continent. Huge stretches of savannah grassland are home to giraffes, rhinos and lions, and elephants roam the bush.

Factfile

- Camels store fat in their humps and can go for a long time without water; they can travel as far as 160 km across the desert in a day.

- The Victoria Falls plunge over a drop of 108 m on the Zambezi River, on the border between Zambia and Zimbabwe.

- Africa's highest mountain, Kilimanjaro, rises to 5,895 m in Tanzania.

- Lake Victoria (69,500 sq km) is Africa's largest lake; Lake Volta (8,482 sq km), in Ghana, is the world's largest artificial lake.

The stone ruins of Great Zimbabwe once enclosed many mud buildings. The oldest parts date from the 700s.

Bake a dough desert

1. Mix smooth dough from six cups of flour, three cups of salt, six tablespoons of cooking oil and water. Roll the dough out, shape it into desert dunes, and then ask an adult to bake it at the bottom of the oven at a low temperature for 40 minutes.

2. When it is cool, paint with PVA glue and sprinkle with real sand. Paint a green oasis, then paint pipe-cleaners green and make them into palm trees. Plant them in lumps of plasticine on the oasis.

Camels are still used by some traders to transport goods across the Sahara desert in North Africa.

Quiz

1 Which country is the world's biggest gold producer?

2 One branch of the Nile is called Blue Nile – what is the other called?

3 What is the cape at the southern tip of Africa called?

4 What is the largest country in Africa?

5 Which is Egypt's (and Africa's) largest city?

6 Niger is an African country; name another by adding two letters.

Answers
1 South Africa.
2 White Nile. 3 Cape of
Good Hope. 4 Sudan.
5 Cairo. 6 Nigeria.

SAY CHEESE!

23

AFRICAN PEOPLE

Scientists believe that the very first humans lived in Africa, millions of years ago. The ancient Egyptian empire began in the north-east of the continent 5,000 years ago. More recently, many African tribes and their lands were controlled by Europeans, but today most African countries are independent. The continent's native peoples still have their own cultures and languages. They traditionally lived in villages and farmed the land, but today there are many growing cities.

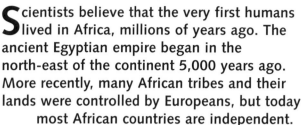

The beaded necklace and headdress is traditional for the Masai tribes of Kenya and Tanzania.

Quiz

1 Which is South Africa's largest city?

2 What is the name of the desert in Namibia?

3 Which African country has the largest population?

4 How many times does the winding River Congo cross the equator?

5 Which famous flat-topped mountain overlooks the city of Cape Town?

6 Does Africa have a larger population than China?

Answers
1 Johannesburg. 2 Namib.
3 Nigeria. 4 Twice.
5 Table Mountain. 6 No.

Johannesburg is the largest city in South Africa with a population of about four million.

Papier-mâché African bangle

1. Cut a cardboard strip about 28 cm long and 3 cm wide. Overlap the ends to fit loosely over the wrist, allowing for the added papier mâché, and tape them together.

2. Mix some PVA glue with water until you have a paste. Tear newspaper into small strips, dip them into the paste and wrap them around the bangle. Cover it with three paper layers. When the papier mâché is dry (it might take a few days), paint the bangle with white paint and then add your own African patterns.

3. For extra effect you could varnish your bangle with clear gloss enamel.

Factfile

- Ostriches are the world's biggest birds and the fastest on land, growing up to 2.5 m tall and running at up to 65 km/h.

- The Suez Canal, in Egypt, is 169 km long; it was opened in 1869 to join the Mediterranean and Red Seas.

- The Mbuti pygmies of central Africa are the world's shortest people; some women are just 1.24 m tall.

- About half a million people live as nomads around the Sahara Desert.

- The Skeleton Coast of Namibia was named because of the many shipwrecks on its shores.

NEWSPAPER STRIPS

GOOD JOB OSTRICHES CAN'T FLY!

AUSTRALASIA

This continent is made up of Australia, New Zealand, Papua New Guinea and thousands of small islands in the South Pacific Ocean. The region is sometimes called Oceania. Australia is much bigger than all the other countries put together. It is a warm, dry country, and much of its land is desert and dry bush, called outback. New Zealand has a milder climate. The warm Pacific Islands cover a vast area, but most of them are very small with few people.

Vanuatu

Samoa

Australia

Fiji

New Caledonia

New Zealand

Factfile

● The roofs of the Sydney Opera House (which opened in 1973) were designed to look like giant sails.

● The Great Barrier Reef is made up of over 2,000 individual coral reefs spread along 2,100 km.

● Sydney was founded in 1788, when the first European settlers arrived in Australia.

● Many Aboriginal rock paintings are thousands of years old. They tell ancient stories.

Geysers and hot springs are common in volcanic regions of New Zealand. In some parts they are used to make electricity.

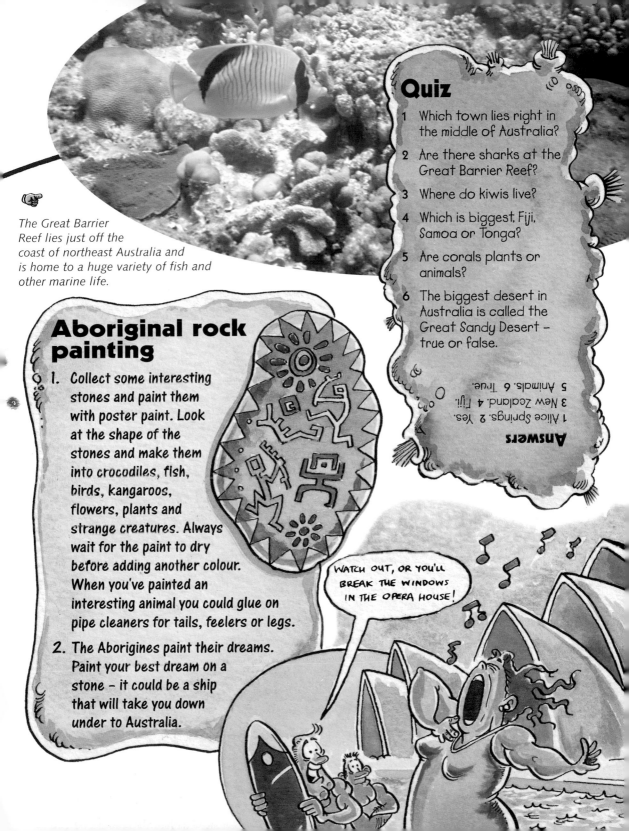

The Great Barrier Reef lies just off the coast of northeast Australia and is home to a huge variety of fish and other marine life.

Quiz

1 Which town lies right in the middle of Australia?

2 Are there sharks at the Great Barrier Reef?

3 Where do kiwis live?

4 Which is biggest, Fiji, Samoa or Tonga?

5 Are corals plants or animals?

6 The biggest desert in Australia is called the Great Sandy Desert – true or false.

Answers
1 Alice Springs. 2 Yes. 3 New Zealand. 4 Fiji. 5 Animals. 6 True.

Aboriginal rock painting

1. Collect some interesting stones and paint them with poster paint. Look at the shape of the stones and make them into crocodiles, fish, birds, kangaroos, flowers, plants and strange creatures. Always wait for the paint to dry before adding another colour. When you've painted an interesting animal you could glue on pipe cleaners for tails, feelers or legs.

2. The Aborigines paint their dreams. Paint your best dream on a stone – it could be a ship that will take you down under to Australia.

WATCH OUT, OR YOU'LL BREAK THE WINDOWS IN THE OPERA HOUSE!

AUSTRALASIAN PEOPLE

The first Australians were Aborigines, who came from Asia about 40,000 years ago. They probably crossed land that is now under water. The first New Zealanders were Maoris, who sailed from the Polynesian islands in about AD800. According to Maori legend, they arrived in just seven canoes. The Pacific islanders themselves sailed from Southeast Asia about 5,000 years ago. In Australia and New Zealand most of the modern inhabitants are descended from European settlers.

Uluru, or Ayers Rock, is a sacred place to the Aborigines. In 1985 it was returned to them to run as a national park with the Australian government.

Quiz

1 Can you go swimming in Lake Eyre?

2 What is the nickname of the Australian rugby union team?

3 Where is the famous Harbour Bridge?

4 On which island does Papua New Guinea lie?

5 What is the capital of Australia?

6 Which country do the Cook Islands belong to?

Answers

1 No (it's normally dry) 2 Wallabies. 3 Sydney. 4 New Guinea. 5 Canberra. 6 New Zealand.

👉 *Wood carving is a traditional craft of the Maoris of New Zealand; they decorate their meeting houses with carvings.*

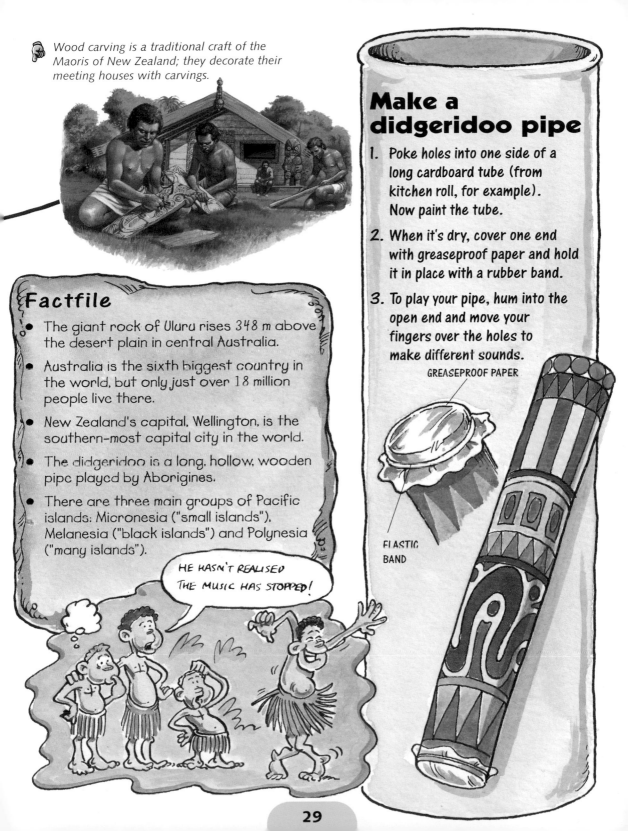

Factfile

- The giant rock of Uluru rises 348 m above the desert plain in central Australia.

- Australia is the sixth biggest country in the world, but only just over 18 million people live there.

- New Zealand's capital, Wellington, is the southern-most capital city in the world.

- The didgeridoo is a long, hollow, wooden pipe played by Aborigines.

- There are three main groups of Pacific islands: Micronesia ("small islands"), Melanesia ("black islands") and Polynesia ("many islands").

HE HASN'T REALISED THE MUSIC HAS STOPPED!

Make a didgeridoo pipe

1. Poke holes into one side of a long cardboard tube (from kitchen roll, for example). Now paint the tube.

2. When it's dry, cover one end with greaseproof paper and hold it in place with a rubber band.

3. To play your pipe, hum into the open end and move your fingers over the holes to make different sounds.

GREASEPROOF PAPER

ELASTIC BAND

ANTARCTICA

The frozen continent of Antarctica lies around the South Pole, at the very bottom of the Earth. The land is covered by a giant icecap, and beneath the ice there are mountains and valleys. No one lives permanently in Antarctica, but there are several bases where scientists work. In winter, temperatures drop to -50°C and there are fierce, freezing winds.

Factfile

- Norwegian explorer Roald Amundsen and his team were the first people to reach the South Pole, in 1911.

- The Transantarctic Mountains stretch for 3,500 km across the entire continent.

- Antarctica means "opposite the Arctic".

- The highest Antarctic mountain is Vinson Massif (5,140 m).

- 90 percent of an iceberg's mass is below the surface of the sea.

Penguins nest in huge colonies called rookeries. They come to land to breed but spend most of their time at sea.

The Amundsen-Scott station stands at the South Pole; a dome protects the buildings inside.

THE UNITED STATES OF AMERICA
WELCOMES YOU TO
AMUNDSEN – SCOTT SOUTH POLE STATION

Quiz

1 Which British explorer was second to reach the South Pole?

2 Do polar bears live in Antarctica?

3 The Ross Ice Shelf is about the size of France – true or false?

4 Which are bigger, emperor penguins or king penguins?

5 What is the name of the imaginary line around the region of Antarctica?

6 Is Antarctica's Mount Erebus a dormant volcano?

Answers

1 Robert Scott 2 No. 3 True.
4 Emperor penguins. 5 Antarctic
Circle. 6 No (it's active).

Ice-cream iceberg

1. Next time you have a party, you could explore the polar regions with your friends.

2. Get a big tub of vanilla ice-cream and stack scoops of ice-cream on a large white plate or tray. Shape the ice-cream into icebergs and ice shelves and sprinkle on coconut. Make a glacier shape with a fork. You could add some ice cubes too.

3. Now give out spoons and get stuck into Antarctica.

EVERYWHERE I LOOK IS NORTH!

SOUTH POLE

ANCIENT EGYPT

Over 5,000 years ago, people settled near the River Nile, in north-east Africa. The ancient Egyptians farmed the fertile land beside their great river. They were ruled by a king, called a pharaoh. They believed that their hawk-god, Horus, entered a new pharaoh and made him a god too. The Egyptians believed in life after death, and pharaohs were buried with things they wanted to take to the next world.

Egyptian queen with two noblewomen.

The Great Pyramid at Giza (one of three large pyramids there) is the only one of the Seven Wonders of the Ancient World still standing.

Hundreds of beautiful golden objects were found in the tomb of the boy-pharaoh Tutankhamun in the Valley of the Kings.

Factfile

- The Great Pyramid is 147 m high; each side of its square base is 230 m long.

- It took about 100,000 men over 20 years to build the Great Pyramid, using more than two million heavy blocks of stone.

- The Egyptians preserved dead bodies by covering them with salt crystals called natron and wrapping them in linen bandages.

- Cats were sacred to the ancient Egyptians, and they worshipped a cat-goddess named Bast.

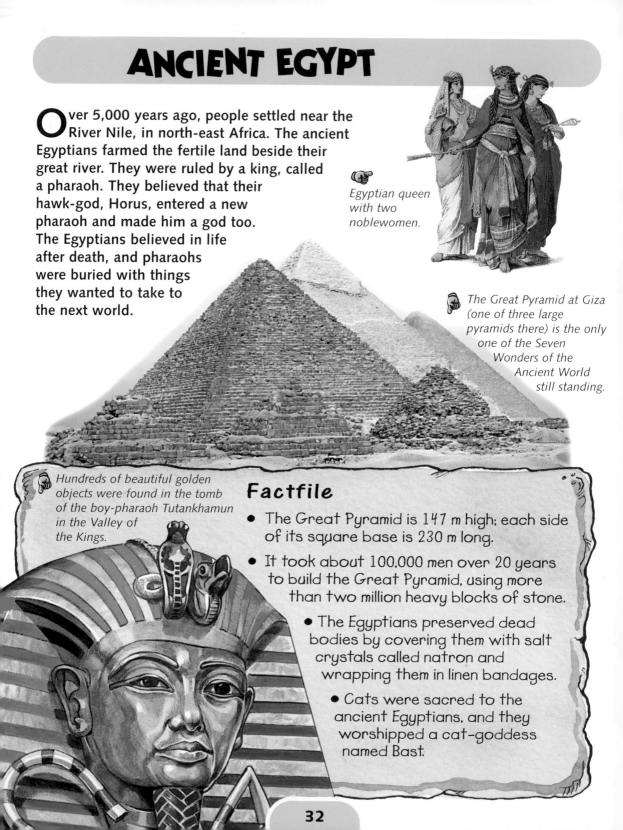

Quiz

1 Which sea does the River Nile flow into?

2 How old was Tutankhamun when he died – 18, 28 or 38?

3 What is the capital of modern Egypt?

4 How tall is the Great Sphinx – 2, 20 or 200 m?

5 What was the name of the Egyptian reed that was used for writing on?

6 The ancient Egyptians were fond of beer – true or false?

Answers

1 Mediterranean. 2 18. 3 Cairo. 4 20 m. 5 Papyrus. 6 True.

Write your name in hieroglyphs

1. The ancient Egyptians invented a system of writing using picture symbols, called hieroglyphs.

2. Use this alphabet to write your own name in hieroglyphs.

A B C D

E F G H

I J K L

M N O P

Q R S T

U V W X

Y Z

DO YOU THINK THE GREAT SPHINX IS A LION WITH A MAN'S HEAD OR A MAN WITH A LION'S BODY?

ANCIENT GREECE

Around 800BC a new civilization developed in Greece. The ancient Greeks produced many fine buildings and built important cities. They wrote great plays and Greek philosophers, or "lovers of wisdom", thought about and discussed important problems and ideas.

 Greek king with his attendants.

The ancient Greeks built the world's first theatres, which were made of stone and built into hillsides.

Quiz

1. Who was the messenger of the Greek gods?
2. Which ancient city is the capital of modern Greece?
3. How many banks of rowers were on each side of a bireme?
4. Which famous temple stands on the Acropolis in Athens?
5. Who was not a philosopher – Plato, Hades, Aristotle?
6. Demeter was the goddess of rain – true or false?

Answers
1 Hermes. 2 Athens. 3 Two. 4 Parthenon.
5 Hades (he was god of the dead).
6 False (she was goddess of grain).

Greek drama mask

1. Cut out a piece of card bigger than your face. Draw on and cut out large eye holes. For a nose fold a piece of card, cut it to shape and glue it on.

2. Cut pieces out of old tights to fit over the eye holes, so people can't see you but you can see them, and glue them into position. Paint the mask white, outline the eyes with black paint and add a happy or a sad mouth. Cut strips of paper for hair and stick them on at the back. Attach a stick to the back of the mask and secure it with parcel tape.

3. Now hold up your mask and face the audience.

Greek warships called triremes had three banks of rowers on each side and were used to ram and sink enemy ships.

Factfile

- The first ancient Olympic Games were held in 776BC at Olympia, a site dedicated to the god Zeus.

- Ancient Greek athletes sometimes carried shields and wore helmets, but no clothes!

- Zeus was king of the Greek gods, and his wife was called Hera.

- In the city state of Sparta, boys were trained to fight from the age of seven.

ANCIENT ROME

The city of Rome began as a small village on one of a group of seven hills, over 2,700 years ago. When the village grew into a city, the Romans conquered other peoples in Italy. Then the Roman army marched further afield to create an empire that stretched around the Mediterranean Sea and as far north as Britain.

Roman general and his standard-bearer.

Roman soldiers built thousands of kilometres of straight roads throughout their empire, and some Roman roads still exist today.

Factfile

- According to legend, Rome was founded in 753BC by two twins, Romulus and Remus, who were raised by a she-wolf.

- Rome was first governed by kings, then it became a republic. Its first emperor, Augustus, took office in 27BC.

- Most Roman gladiators were slaves who had been captured in war.

- The Colosseum in Rome was completed in AD80. It could hold about 50,000 spectators.

Gladiators fought to the death for the amusement of the huge crowds. Other shows included men fighting against animals such as lions, rhinos and bears.

BE GENTLE!

Quiz

1 What do we call the structures that brought water into Roman cities?

2 What was the name of the main square in ancient Rome?

3 What was a Roman officer who commanded 100 soldiers called?

4 Which famous Roman was murdered on the Ides of March?

5 Which Roman emperor built a wall to keep Scottish tribes out?

6 Did Asterix and Obelix really exist?

Answers
1 Aqueducts. 2 The Forum.
3 Centurion. 4 Julius
Caesar 5 Hadrian. 6 No.

The Italian town of Pompeii was buried under volcanic ash when nearby Mount Vesuvius erupted in AD79

Match the Roman soldiers

Roman soldiers wore different uniforms and carried different weapons according to their rank and the sort of fighting they did.

Can you spot which two in the row of soldiers below are exactly the same?

THE MIDDLE AGES

The Middle Ages is the name usually given to a period of history that started in about AD500 and lasted for around a thousand years. We think of the period before the Middle Ages as ancient history, and afterwards as modern times. During the Middle Ages European countries were ruled by kings and emperors who generally owned the land. They divided it among their most important men, called nobles. The nobles were supported by knights, who were trained to fight. Peasants farmed the land, growing food for their families and their lord.

Henry VI and VII with members of the Court.

Medieval kings and nobles built castles to protect themselves from enemies.

Quiz

1 What were mechanical bows that shot bolts called?

2 What was tapped on a squire's shoulder to make him a knight?

3 What was the name of a medieval entertainer who clowned around?

4 Which famous city did the Crusaders conquer in 1099?

5 What was the water surrounding a castle called?

6 Which weapon did knights use for jousting?

Answers
1 Crossbows. 2 Sword. 3 Jester. 4 Jerusalem. 5 Moat. 6 Lance.

Factfile

- In medieval towns there were no proper drains, so people threw their rubbish and emptied their pots into the street.

- A terrible plague called the Black Death spread from Asia to Europe in the 1300s and killed at least a third of the population.

- For a period of almost 200 years, from 1095, Christian knights went on Crusades to win back the Holy Land from Muslim rulers.

Make a stained-glass window

1. Draw a window frame on a piece of thick black paper and cut it out. You can make up your own frame and designs, but they should be big enough so that you can cut them out easily.

2. Place a sheet of tracing paper on the table, the same size as your window. Glue or tape the frame onto the decorated tracing paper and arrange small pieces of coloured tissue paper or cellophane on it. Apply tiny dabs of glue to stick on the coloured pieces.

3. Hang the stained glass up in your window and watch the colours light up when the sun shines through.

LANGUAGES OF THE WORLD

Language is made up of the words we speak or write down. Words help us to communicate with each other, to tell each other things. There are thousands of different languages all over the world, as well as different alphabets for writing them down. Most people grow up speaking just one language, called their mother tongue, but they often learn other foreign languages when they are older.

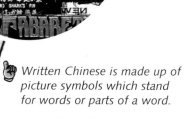

Say hello to over 1,400 million people!

There are about 4,000 different languages spoken in the world! This is how to write and say hello in just eight of them.

FRENCH

Hello - **Bonjour**
(bon - shoor)

ITALIAN

Hello - **Ciao**
(chow)

RUSSIAN

Hello - **Здравствуйте**
(zdras - vid - ye)

MANDARIN

Hello - 你好
(nee - how)

JAPANESE

Hello - こんにちは
(kon - nich - ee - wah)

HEBREW

Hello - שלום
(sha - lom)

ARABIC

Hello - أهلا
(eh - lun)

SWAHILI

Hello - **Jambo**
(jam - bow)

Written Chinese is made up of picture symbols which stand for words or parts of a word.

NOW, ONE OF THESE IS OUR HOTEL !!

Quiz

1 What is the main language of Quebec, in Canada?

2 In which country is Urdu the official language?

3 What are the two main languages of Switzerland?

4 What do Italians call Rome?

5 Arabic is written from right to left – true or false?

6 What is the most frequently used letter in written English?

Answers
1 French. 2 Pakistan.
3 French and German.
4 Roma. 5 True. 6 E.

IT'LL NEVER CATCH ON!

Factfile

- Mandarin Chinese is the most spoken language in the world, followed by English and Hindi (the main official language of India).

- Russian has its own alphabet, which came originally from Greek; it has 33 letters.

- The international flag code has a different flag for all 26 letters of the English alphabet, and is still sometimes used by sailors.

- Holy Roman Emperor Charles V (1500–58) is said to have spoken French to men, Italian to women, German to horses and Spanish to God.

- There are about 1,300 languages in Africa alone.

The Rosetta stone is an ancient carved stone slab that was discovered in 1799. It was used to decipher Egyptian hieroglyphics, which before then modern people could not understand.

41

RELIGIONS

Religion has been practised in different ways in all known civilizations from the earliest times. The world's main modern religions have existed for thousands of years, trying to explain the world and the meaning and purpose of life to their believers. It is thought that more than three-quarters of the world's people follow some form of religion. The religions and their followers have a lot in common.

Hindu gods and goddesses have been worshipped in India and neighbouring countries for thousands of years.

Factfile

- Jerusalem is a holy city for Muslims, Jews and Christians.

- Hinduism is a major religion in India and neighbouring countries; it is thousands of years old.

- Christianity has about 1,930 million followers; Islam about 1,100 million; Hinduism about 780 million; and Buddhism about 325 million.

- Shintoism, the ancient religion of Japan, has about 120 million followers.

- The Sikh religion began in India over 500 years ago; Sikhs follow the lessons of teachers called gurus.

I BRING FRANKINCENSE, BUT MUM SAYS CAN SHE HAVE THE JAR BACK!

Match the symbols to the religions

1. All religions have special symbols which mean a great deal to their followers.

2. Can you match these five symbols to the right religions? The answers are below.

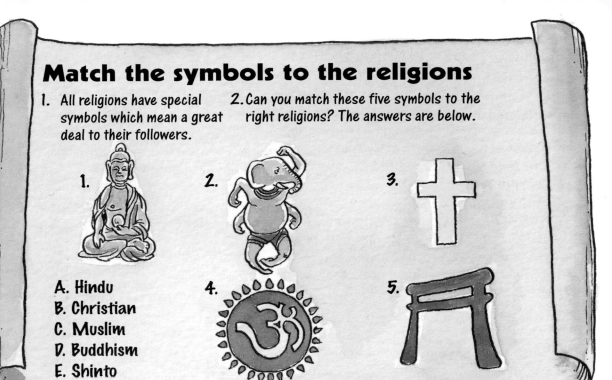

1.

2.

3.

4.

5.

A. Hindu
B. Christian
C. Muslim
D. Buddhism
E. Shinto

Religious symbols: 1D, 2A, 3B, 4C, 5E.

Quiz

1 In which city is the Muslim Temple called the Dome of the Rock?

2 Which Church is the Pope head of?

3 What is the name of the head covering worn by Sikhs?

4 Which Indian river is sacred to Hindus?

5 Which city do Muslims face when they pray?

6 What is a Jewish place of worship called?

Answers
1 Jerusalem. 2 Roman Catholic Church. 3 Turban. 4 Ganges. 5 Mecca. 6 Synagogue.

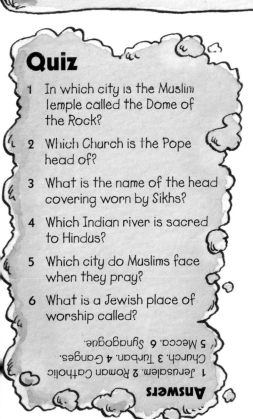

The Wailing Wall is a holy site for all Jews. It was part of the Temple of Jerusalem which was first built by King Solomon in 950BC. After being destroyed in 586BC, the Temple was re-built and again destroyed. The Wailing Wall is now part of the Muslim Dome of the Rock.

43

FESTIVALS AND CUSTOMS

There are thousands of different festivals all over the world. They mostly celebrate a person or an event, and many of them happen once a year on special days called holidays. Many holidays, or "holy days", are linked with religion, such as Christian Easter, Islamic Eid Al-Fittr and Hindu Holi. Many festivals and religions have given rise to special customs and traditions, which are kept alive by being handed down from one generation to the next.

Piñata game

The piñata is a Mexican toy full of goodies.

1. Stuff a paper bag with scrunched-up newspaper to make it firm, and then tie it with string. Paint and decorate the bag. Screw up pieces of tissue paper, cut strips of crêpe paper and paste them on. Untie the bag, take out the newspaper and fill it with sweets. Retie the string and ask an adult to hang your piñata from the ceiling.

2. Blindfold a player, give him or her a rolled-up newspaper and let them have a go at knocking down the piñata. Each player can have three attempts and then it's the next person's turn. When somebody knocks the piñata down, share the sweets out among everyone.

Dragon dancers weave through the streets, celebrating Chinese New Year.

44

The annual carnival in Rio de Janeiro, Brazil, is the most famous in the world.

Quiz

1 Which food do people traditionally make on Shrove Tuesday?

2 Which special Wednesday follows Shrove Tuesday?

3 Which saint is also called Santa Claus?

4 In Japan there are two doll festivals, one for girls and one for boys – true or false?

5 What is the alternative to a treat at Halloween?

6 When is Russian Christmas Day?

Answers
1 Pancakes. 2 Ash Wednesday. 3 St Nicholas. 4 True. 5 A trick. 6 6 January.

Factfile

● Halloween, celebrated on 31 October, is a shortening of All Hallows Eve, or "the day before the feast of All Saints".

● The Hindus of India and Nepal like to play tricks during their spring festival of Holi, such as throwing coloured powder and water at each other.

● In northern Europe people traditionally dance around the maypole on 1 May to celebrate the coming of spring.

● Some people think that the year 2000 is the last year of the old century and millennium rather than the first year of the new century and millennium.

SPORTS

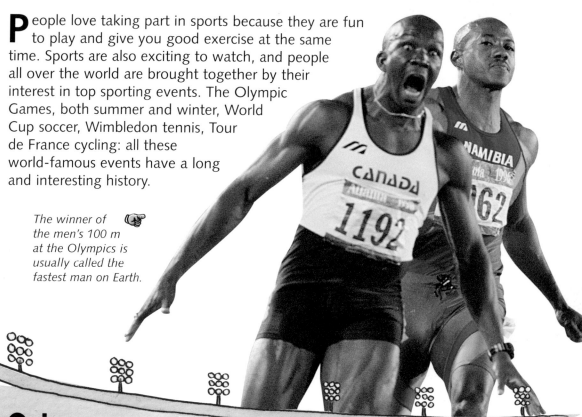

People love taking part in sports because they are fun to play and give you good exercise at the same time. Sports are also exciting to watch, and people all over the world are brought together by their interest in top sporting events. The Olympic Games, both summer and winter, World Cup soccer, Wimbledon tennis, Tour de France cycling: all these world-famous events have a long and interesting history.

The winner of the men's 100 m at the Olympics is usually called the fastest man on Earth.

Quiz

1 How many events are there in the decathlon?

2 Do female gymnasts perform on the rings?

3 Which city do the Yankees baseball team come from?

4 What colour jersey does the Tour de France leader wear?

5 Which country has won most Olympic gold medals?

6 Which martial art means "kick-punch-method"?

SORRY!

Answers
1 Ten. 2 No.
3 New York. 4 Yellow.
5 USA. 6 Taekwondo.

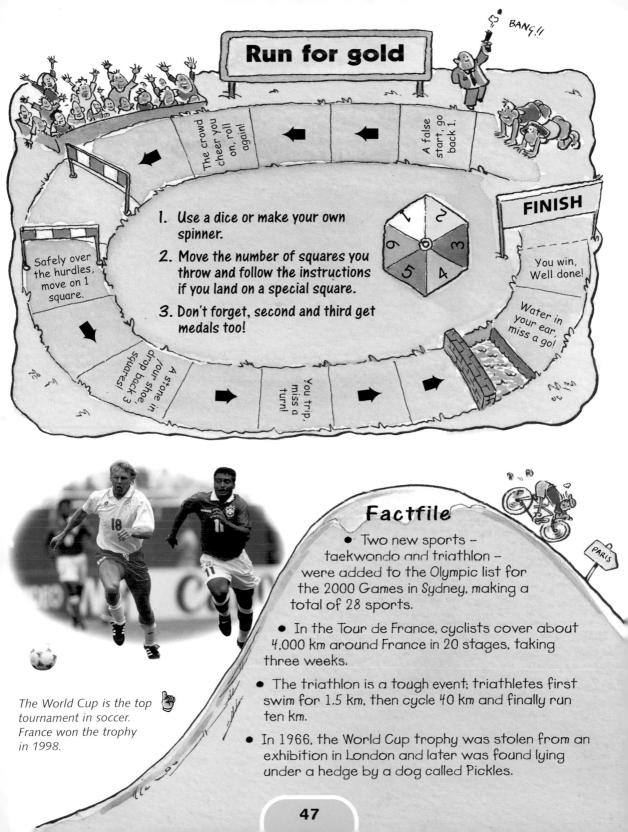

Run for gold

BANG!!

The crowd cheer you on, roll again!

A false start, go back 1.

FINISH

Safely over the hurdles, move on 1 square.

You win, Well done!

Water in your ear, miss a go!

1. Use a dice or make your own spinner.

2. Move the number of squares you throw and follow the instructions if you land on a special square.

3. Don't forget, second and third get medals too!

A stone in your shoe, drop back 3 squares!

You trip, miss a turn!

The World Cup is the top tournament in soccer. France won the trophy in 1998.

Factfile

- Two new sports – taekwondo and triathlon – were added to the Olympic list for the 2000 Games in Sydney, making a total of 28 sports.

- In the Tour de France, cyclists cover about 4,000 km around France in 20 stages, taking three weeks.

- The triathlon is a tough event; triathletes first swim for 1.5 km, then cycle 40 km and finally run ten km.

- In 1966, the World Cup trophy was stolen from an exhibition in London and later was found lying under a hedge by a dog called Pickles.

PARIS

Index